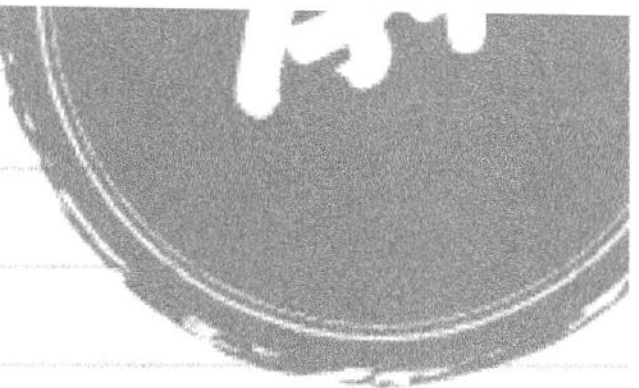

SIGNS OF A NARCISSIST

How to recognize a narcissist

Written by Yvonnie Davis

Hello Dear Reader I am Yvonnie the writer of this eBook. I am a divorced 39 year old mother of 4. After my divorce I entered back into the dating world and just let me say this; there are some characters out here! When dating you come in contact with all types of people! Some are a little touched in the head, and some are completely off there rockers! It may sound funny, but I'm being serious! It's a mad house out there, and there will be times you say "You know what, I'm good with being single! Me personally I'm at the point where I just want to chill and focus on me! However I know there are some people still out here searching for Mr./Mrs. Right, and along the way they are going to run into Mr./Mrs.

Narcissist and I want them to be prepared, which is the reason I wrote this ebook! I don't want you to be blindsided by them, because ooh wee that wouldn't be fair at all! So I am here to save you some stress, and strands of hair.

Now in order to identify a person with a narcissist mindset you have to know what a narcissist is defined as;

Narcissistic personality disorder is a disorder which a person has an inflated sense of self importance, low regards for other people's feelings , have a hard time handling criticism and have a high sense of entitlement! Now this is a small description of a narcissist mindset, and just by that how many of you think you have met or are with a narcissist? You probably have been trying to figure out what the hell was wrong with them this entire time, and then again they probably had you convinced that you were the one with issues! That's something they do too! They gaslight you, make you feel guilty and portray themselves as the victim! If you aren't a sharp thinker they will mind fuck you, excuse my language but they will!

#1. Now a narcissist will seem like the perfect, sweetest, most likable person at first. They may go out of their way to be helpful in some unideal situations, people are going to tell you how good of a person they are convincing you that you have found yourself a winner! Am I right? Ok keep reading! They may profess their love early in the relationship and may try to rush you into a serious commitment before you are ready! While you may be cautious, you will be convinced that you have found the person you have been looking for, who's also ready for the commitment you have been searching for! Don't mistake this for love and romance, because it's only a way for them to gain control! So Run!!!!!!!

#2 They constantly talk about themselves, because they are the center of the world in their eyes. No matter the topic of discussion it's always going to be about them and how they feel! They aren't concerned with your opinions or feelings, because the lack of empathy they have is ridiculous So don't bother explaining anything from your point of view, because you will be wasting your time! Simply put they don't care about anyone's feelings except their own!

#3 They hate criticism, or their flaws to be mentioned. If you bring up anything about them besides praises there will be hell to pay! They will not acknowledge or take into consideration to change. All they're going to do is jump all over you in defense mode, because they view themselves as everything except for a problem. If you're discussing a current issue or problem, they're going to bring up something you did in the past to avoid you talking about them and to shift the blame! This is to avoid fixing any present problems that you're experiencing. This is so you will get tired of debating it and give up the fight!

#4 They build you up only to break you down! They compliment you and criticize you at the same time! They may say I like that dress, but it would look better if you weren't so big. It's a method to lower your self esteem and to have you self conscious about yourself! It plays a role in their sick twisted plot to ensure that you never leave their sadistic

abusive ass! You willing
feel like nobody else will
want you!

#5 They don't like/
can't stand rejection. This is a
sure fire
            way to piss them off.
They feel like they're superior to
you and
            and everyone else so
when you reject them that same
charm

they displayed in the beginning the total opposite! They pout and give you the silent treatment until they aren't mad anymore! You're basically dealing with a child! If you decide to leave a narcissist the situation will more than likely become violent because they can't take no for an answer sometimes!

#6 They play the victim after continuously victimizing you.

They will belittle you, criticize everything you say or do, talk

to you crazy
repeatedly, but the moment you
speak up or
          speak on them or
stuff about them they all of a
sudden they
          become a victim! All
of a sudden you're mean and
treating
          them bad! Because as
I stated they only care about
          themselves. They
have no regards for your feelings
honestly!

They start
mentioning past trauma and
anything else to make
themselves a victim,
in order to excuse their crap.

#7 They take everything as a threat: they will misinterpret facial expressions or body language! They make it negative!

You may wake up and if you look a certain way they automatically jump in defense mode! You may even say I love

you or even apologize and it will piss them off! They may take

a simple joke as a form of a personal attack on them because

in their minds everything is about them!

#8 they gaslight you
and make it seem like you're
overreacting when
you tell them they are upsetting
you or

making you feel
some type of way because of
how they're
treating you. They
make your feelings small and

unimportant; and
expect you to be cool their
abuse, then get
                mad when you're not!

#9 They will exploit people for their own benefit! It doesn't matter if it's their significant other or family and friends. It

may sound like this should be obvious, but narcissists are

master manipulators. They have sensed your needs and

desires as well as your soft spot/ weakness! They have

handpicked you to
exploit or use, and they do it
with no
remorse because
they don't care about or love you
in any
type of way.

#10 They are pathological liars! We all lie to a certain extent.

They lie even when the truth won't cause any harm though.

Then have to lie more to keep the story alive! They con you

into believing the bs, even though you know without a

shadow of a doubt that they full of crap.

#11 The lack of accountability they possess is unreal! They will lie, shift the blame or anything they can pull to get away with murder! They will not accept the blame for shit

even if it would
save their life! Somehow they will blame
you for the shit
that do even if you had nothing to do with
it. This is because
causing you to question your sanity is
more entertaining
to them!

#12 They constantly try to make you feel like you're not

good enough no matter what you do. They will brag on

other people as if they're trying to compare you to them,

and if you do they will call you crazy for trying to compete!

#13 Your needs
are always ignored. They only
think about

themselves and what they want . Even if they want it too!

Simply because you want it it's a problem. Especially sex!

You better not even think about doing them that way

though! Because if you do welcome to a war zone!!

#14 Reverts to child like behavior when they can't get their way such as the silent treatment. This is a form of control. They ignore you, aren't affectionate until they

feel like it or
want something! They will play
nice then
because they
want something! After dealing
with it for
so long you may
start to feel like this is normal;
well let
me tell you it's
not!

#15 They refuse to admit or change their behavior! This is because in their eyes nothing is wrong with them.

They know that if they agree to change, they'll be admitting they have a problem and that isn't happening.

Conclusion

Now while there are many signs of a narcissist these are some that I have personally experienced. At first I was clueless to the type of shit I was dealing with; then I did my research. It is rough dealing with a person with these tendencies. It is a constant battle; you are tired, wore out crying, depressed all the time! You trying to explain your feelings but it doesn't get better! Narcissist will mistreat you as long as you allow them to! It's hard to walk away sometimes, because in the beginning they make you feel loved and appreciated, they treat you good and once you're hooked, they flip on you! You're sitting there trying to fix whatever you have to in order to get the person they once were back; it's not going to happen though! They gradually broke you down piece by piece, lowered your self esteem, made you question your self worth, and even made you feel like you were going to be in a worse situation if you left! Now you're to full of fear to walk away. If you're at this point my advice to you is to pray, seek therapy, and gain the strength you need to get out! If you're in fear for your safety you need to seek some assistance to move forward with a proper plan to leave as soon as possible! So many people have lost their lives, or freedom over things like this and it's time to break the cycle! I really hope this has helped someone bring enlightenment to a stressful situation I pray you're able to move on safely! God bless!!

Chapter 1

Now in order to identify a person with a narcissist mindset , you have to know what a narcissist is defined as! So here you go; Narcissistic personality disorder is a disorder which a person has an inflated sense of self importance, low regards for other people's feelings, they have a hard time handling criticism (but can easily give it out), and a high sense of entitlement. Now this is a small definition or description of a narcissistic mindset, and by that how many of you think you have met or are with one. You probably were trying to figure out what the hell was wrong with them this entire time, but then again they probably convinced you that you were the problem! See that's something that they do too! They make you feel like you're the one in the wrong and they are innocent! Honestly if you aren't a sharp thinker, they will mind fuck you! I'm sorry but cautious, you will be convinced that you have found the person you have been looking for, who's also ready for the commitment you have been searching for!

Don't mistake this for love and
romance, because it's only a
way for them to gain control!
So Run!!!!!!!

About the Author

Yvonnie Davis

www.ingramcontent.com/pod-product-compliance
Lightning Source LLC
Chambersburg PA
CBHW072110150726
47999CB00005B/1989